Life in the
Tropical Forests

Life in the Tropical Forests

Salvatore Tocci

Watts LIBRARY™

Franklin Watts
A Division of Scholastic Inc.
New York • Toronto • London • Auckland • Sydney
Mexico City • New Delhi • Hong Kong
Danbury, Connecticut

For Mary Jo and all the memories that will never fade

Note to readers: Definitions for words in **bold** can be found in the Glossary at the back of this book.

Photographs © 2005: Corbis Images: 29 (Dave Bartruff), 22 (Gary Braasch), 18 (Macduff Everton), 43 (Martin Harvey), 34 bottom (Lindsay Hebberd), cover (Wolfgang Kaehler), 26 (David Muench), 31 (Carl & Ann Purcell), 19 (Anders Ryman); Corbis Sygma/Herve Collart: 8, 9, 36; Minden Pictures: 44 (Michael & Patricia Fogden), 2, 32, 39, 47, 48, 50 (Frans Lanting), 41 (Tom Mangelsen), 34 top (Mark Moffett), 46 (Konrad Wothe), 28 (Norbert Wu); NASA: 21 (Jacques Descloitres/MODIS Rapid Respnse Team/GSFC); Peter Arnold Inc.: 35 (Compost/Visage), 6 (Mark Edwards), 42 (Michel Gunther), 15 (Luiz C. Marigo), 14 (Claus Meyer), 16 (David Woodfall/WWI); Photo Researchers, NY: 5 bottom, 40 (Tom & Pat Leeson), 24, 25 (Dr. Morely Read), 5 top, 10 (Martin Wendler); PhotoEdit/Tom Carter: 51; Visuals Unlimited/Dr. E. F. Anderson: 53.

Illustrations by: Bob Italiano

The photograph on the cover shows the lush tropical rain forest vegetation on Atiu Island, Cook Islands. The photograph opposite the title page shows a stream running through Tropical Cloud Forest in Costa Rica.

Library of Congress Cataloging-in-Publication Data

Tocci, Salvatore.
  Life in the tropical forests / Salvatore Tocci.— 1st ed.
      p. cm.
  Includes bibliographical references and index.
  ISBN 0-531-12364-2
  1. Forest ecology—Tropics—Juvenile literature. I. Title.
  QH84.5.T59 2005
  577.34—dc22   2004027054

Contents

This child belongs to a tribe of people called the Yanomami, a word that means "human being."

The Yanomami

The Yanomami are a tribe of people who live in hundreds of small villages along both sides of the border between Brazil and Venezuela. The Yanomami have lived in South America for perhaps as long as one thousand years. Only a few people outside the region, however, knew that the Yanomami even existed until recently. In the 1980s, gold was discovered on their land. In their search for fortune, tens of thousands of people from all over the world flocked to the land

where the Yanomami once lived unnoticed by the outside world.

How could the Yanomami have remained isolated from the rest of the world for so long? The answer can be found by

looking at where these people live. From the closest port, it takes seven days traveling by boat, canoe, and foot to reach a Yanomami village. These villages are located deep in a type of forest that grows in only certain parts of the world.

Tropical forests are home to more than half of all the types of plants and animals that live on Earth.

Chapter One

The World's Tropical Forests

The Yanomami live in a **tropical forest,** which people commonly call a jungle. Scientists also call it a tropical rain forest. This name reveals one way in which a tropical forest is different from other types of forests. A tropical forest gets much more rain.

The tropical forest is one of the world's **biomes.** Scientists divide the world into various biomes. Each biome is an area on Earth where environmental conditions determine the types of plants and animals that can live there. These conditions include how much sunlight and rain the region receives.

Along the Equator

Tropical forests are found along the equator, which is an imaginary line around the middle of Earth. Only this part of the world has the environmental conditions that a tropical forest needs to grow. One of these conditions is plenty of rain. Each year, a tropical forest gets at least 65 inches (165 centimeters) of rain. Compare this with a desert, which may receive less than 0.5 inch (1.3 cm) of rain per year. The rain must not only be plentiful, but it must also fall in sufficient amounts throughout the year. At least 4 inches (10 cm) of rain must fall each month to support the growth of a tropical forest.

A second environmental condition is a warm temperature throughout the year. Daytime temperatures in a tropical forest remain close to 80 degrees Fahrenheit (27 degrees Celsius) year round. Even at night the temperature never drops below freezing. As a result, the average daily temperature remains about 65° F (18° C). The combination of warm temperature and high rainfall results in constant high humidity.

Most of the tropical forests are in the Americas, including the Caribbean, Mexico, and Central and South America. The largest is the Amazon forest, which stretches across South

The Record

More than 86 feet (26 meters) of rain fell in one year on a tropical forest in India.

America for about 2,000 miles (3,219 kilometers). Most of the Amazon forest is in Brazil.

The second largest area covered by tropical forests is in central Africa, mainly in the Democratic Republic of Congo. The third and smallest area of tropical forests is in Asia, including India, Indonesia, and the Philippines. All together, tropical forests cover about 4.5 million square miles (11.7 million square km) of land. In comparison, the United States covers about 3.6 million square miles (9.3 million sq km).

Surviving in the Forest

Isolated from the rest of the world, the Yanomami depend entirely on the tropical forest to survive. Each Yanomami village actually consists of just one building, which is called a *yano*. From above, a yano looks like a giant doughnut. The building is large, with a diameter about the length of a football field.

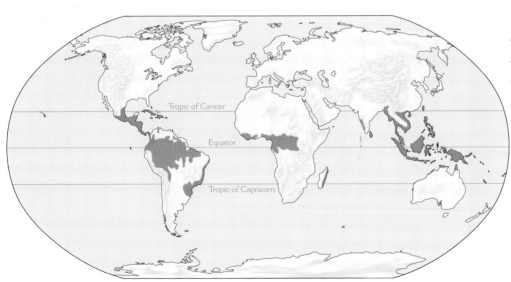

Tropical forests are located around the Earth near the equator.

13

The building has a roof made from vines and the leaves of palm trees. As many as four hundred Yanomami may live in the circular building.

The Yanomami are farmers and hunters. They grow up to twenty different crops, including sweet potatoes, bananas, and corn. The crops provide about 80 percent of their food. The remaining 20 percent comes from hunting, although some Yanomami fish. Hunting is done by the males, who start learning hunting skills when they are as young as five years old.

A Disappearing People

No one is quite sure how long the Yanomami have lived in the tropical forests because, until recently, very few other people knew they existed. The Yanomami live in harmony with the forest. The forest supports them. In turn, they respect the forest by making sure to take only what they need to survive. Since gold was discovered on their land, however, the Yanomami population has been in decline.

Yanomami villages slowly disappeared as trees were cut down to make way for landing strips so that prospectors, people looking for gold, could fly into the region rather than hike through the forest. The prospectors also brought diseases, such as malaria and tuberculosis. The Yanomami had no natural resistance to these diseases, because they had never been exposed to them before the prospectors arrived.

The Yanomami will hunt only for what they need to survive.

Since 1987, one in ten Yanomami has died from a disease brought to the region by prospectors. Those who survive face starvation as their food sources gradually disappear because the forests are cleared. No one is sure how many Yanomami are living today. Sadly, the Yanomami are not the only living things disappearing from the tropical forests.

The tropical forest in which the Yanomami live contains diamonds, gold, and other valuable minerals.

A Yanomami Speaks

In 1990, a Yanomami leader told an interviewer about the impact contact with outsiders has had on his people's way of life, "In the beginning our health was good, we didn't die in droves, we didn't suffer from malaria. We hunted, we had celebrations, we were happy. Today, the Yanomami do not even build their yanos; they just live in little huts in the forest, under plastic sheeting. They don't even plant vegetable gardens [or] go hunting anymore, because they are always sick. That's the way it is."

These tropical forest trees were cut down and burned to clear the land for farmland and grazing pasture.

Chapter Two

A Disappearing Biome

Deep in the Amazon forest grow some of the most valuable trees in the world. They are known as big leaf mahogany trees. Each tree can be worth as much as $100,000. But the tree must first be chopped down and cut into lumber. Mahogany wood is prized for its color and durability. The wood is used to make musical instruments and furniture,

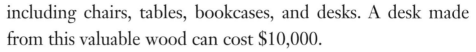

including chairs, tables, bookcases, and desks. A desk made from this valuable wood can cost $10,000.

The value of these mahogany trees has lured many loggers into the Amazon forest. Trees along riverbanks, which are the easiest to reach, have been completely stripped. Between 1971 and 1990, an estimated 600,000 mahogany trees were cut down in the Amazon forest.

The damage to the forest caused by logging extends far beyond the number of mahogany trees that have been cut down. Mahogany trees are scattered throughout the forest, with an average of only one tree every 2.5 acres (1 hectare). Loggers often bulldoze other trees to build access roads that stretch for hundreds of miles to reach a single mahogany tree.

A Ban

In 2001, the Brazilian government banned the logging of its mahogany trees.

This man is burning a tract of forestland for his farm.

Slash and Burn

To plant their crops, the Yanomami first had to clear the land of trees and brush. They began by cutting down trees and other tall plants. Then they burned the land to clear out any remaining vegetation. This process of clearing the land is known as slash and burn.

The Yanomami slashed and burned just enough of the forest to plant their crops. The soil in tropical forests, how-

ever, is not good for growing crops. The soil is poor in **nutrients,** which are substances living things need to survive and grow. After two or three years, the Yanomami would have to move to a new location and repeat their slash-and-burn process. Trees and other plants would slowly start to grow in the area they had abandoned.

Today, slash and burn is still used to clear tropical forestland for agriculture. The areas that are being cleared

The cleared area on the hillside was burned by farmers so the land could be used to harvest rice.

are far larger than what the Yanomami slashed and burned, however. In the mid-1960s, Brazil launched Operation Amazonia. This operation involved almost 2 million square miles (5.18 million sq km), which is about half the size of the continental United States. Much of the Amazon forest was to be cleared to make way for farmland for five million families.

The Brazilian government promised to build more than 9,000 miles (14,484 km) of roads through the forest. The longest road was named the Transamazon Highway, which eventually extended more than 3,000 miles (4,828 km). The goal of Operation Amazonia was to give each family 250 acres (101.3 ha) along these highways for its farm. Between 1970 and 1974, however, fewer than five thousand people settled along these roads. Like the Yanomami, most families found the soil too poor to farm and left the region. Today, parts of the Transamazon Highway are abandoned, and other sections have been washed away by heavy rains. The highway may be gone, but the damage it caused to the Amazon forest remains.

Tropical forests in other parts of the world have suffered the same fate. In 1997, the smoke from slash-and-burn fires in Indonesia reduced visibility for hundreds of miles. Flights traveling into the region, including flights to places as far away as Singapore and the Philippines, had to be canceled. Children and the elderly had to remain indoors for days because the fires caused such bad breathing problems.

Tavy

For centuries, the people of Madagascar, an island off the east coast of Africa, practiced a slash-and-burn technique they called tavy. Like the Yanomami, they cut and burned only enough trees to plant their crops. After two or three years, they moved on and returned to an area only when the soil had regained enough nutrients. As the population grew, however, they could no longer wait for used areas to recover and were forced to clear new areas. As a result, less than 5 percent of the original tropical forest of Madagascar exists today.

The red band in this satellite photograph represents the slash-and-burn fires spreading across the tropical forests of Africa.

Cattle Ranchers

One estimate states that 6 square yards (5 square m) of tropical forests are destroyed for every 4-ounce (114-gram) hamburger that is eaten.

The same year that fires were burning in Indonesia, slash-and-burn fires were also pouring smoke into the air above the Amazon forest in Brazil. Over a period of three months near the end of 1997, some 45,000 separate fires were counted with the help of satellite images. The combined

slash-and-burn fires in Indonesia and Brazil represented the largest area on Earth to be on fire at any one time in recorded history.

The fires in Brazil had been set not only by farmers but also by ranchers, who were being encouraged by the Brazilian government to settle in the Amazon forest. Beginning in the 1970s, the demand for beef started increasing dramatically worldwide. This demand came mainly from fast-food chains that needed hamburger meat.

To supply this increased demand for beef, huge areas of the Amazon forest were cleared for cattle ranches. By 1980, these ranches were responsible for clearing nearly three-quarters of the forest that had been destroyed in Brazil. But establishing cattle ranches is not an easy task. Heavy rains often wash away the grass seed that is planted. Even when grass does grow, the nutrient-poor soil limits how long cattle can graze on the land. An area usually cannot be grazed for more than five years. The ranchers then have to move and clear a new area for their cattle.

Number One

Brazil has the largest number of cattle in the world.

The World Impact

Tropical forests cover only 6 percent of Earth's surface. But their destruction—whether for logging, farming, or ranching—affects the whole world. You read how the smoke from the slash-and-burn fires in Indonesia affected neighboring parts of the world. Such fires may eventually affect other parts of the world.

Scientists think that because of the destruction of tropical forests, dozens of different kinds of animals and plants become extinct every day.

Burning releases gases into the **atmosphere.** One of these gases is carbon dioxide. Most of this carbon dioxide comes from the burning of coal and gasoline. But the burning of tropical forests also releases a significant amount of carbon dioxide. All this carbon dioxide, along with other gases, collects in the atmosphere above Earth where it contributes to **global warming.**

Global warming is the warming of Earth because of the presence of gases in the atmosphere that trap heat energy from the sun. Trapping this heat energy causes a gradual increase in Earth's average annual temperature. An increase in Earth's temperature will gradually melt the polar glaciers, causing sea levels to rise. Scientists estimate that sea levels may rise from 4 to 35 inches (10 to 89 cm) by the year 2100. This rise in sea level would affect billions of people who live in coastal cities and communities.

Global warming is not the only problem associated with burning tropical forests. Compared with all other biomes, tropical forests contain the greatest diversity of living things. No one is sure how many different types of plants and animals live on Earth. Some estimate as many as 100 million different kinds of living things exist, most of which have not been identified. As many as ninety million of these may live in tropical forests. Many that live in tropical forests live nowhere else on Earth. Destroying tropical forests will lead to the extinction of countless numbers of plants and animals.

A big leaf mahogany tree grows to be 120 feet (37 m) tall and 6 feet (1.8 m) in diameter.

Chapter Three

Plants: From Top to Bottom

The Yanomami use about six hundred different types of plants. They eat some plants and use others to build their community shelter. The Yanomami extract dyes from certain plants to decorate their faces and bodies for ceremonies. They also use many plants as medicines, including ones to treat infections, pain, and wounds. Let's take a look at some of

A Huge
Umbrella

The leaves of an
emergent tree can
spread over an acre
of land.

*Lianas can grow to be
thicker than an adult
human body.*

the plants that grow only in a tropical forest, starting at the top.

The Emergent Trees

With plenty of rain and warm temperatures, plants can grow all year round in a tropical forest. As a result, some trees grow to be 200 feet (61 m) high, or as tall as a twenty-story building. These giants are known as emergent trees, because they emerge, or rise, above everything else in a tropical forest.

Standing so tall, emergent trees are in the best position to receive sunlight. Plants depend on the energy they get from sunlight to carry out **photosynthesis,** which is the process they use to make food. The height of the emergent trees, however, also has its disadvantages. Emergent trees are exposed to the high winds that sometimes blow through a tropical forest. The roots of emergent trees are shallow, but the roots spread out over a wide area to help anchor the tree in the ground. Huge vines grow up from the ground and also help stabilize the trees. Wrapping itself around a tree, a vine can

28

grow as long as 800 feet (244 m). These vines, known as lianas, give the tropical forest its jungle look.

Despite the support they get from their roots and lianas, emergent trees are sometimes knocked down by hurricane-force winds. A lightning strike may also topple an emergent tree. When an emergent tree falls, it usually brings down dozens of other trees with it. What remains is a huge area open to the sky, known as a light gap. This gap allows more sunlight to reach the lower layers of the tropical forest.

The Canopy

Beneath the tops of the emergent trees is a thick, green umbrella of leaves known as a **canopy.** The word *canopy* means "covering." True to its name, the canopy forms a dense cover over much of the tropical forest. In contrast with

The canopy is home to many tropical forest animals that range in size from tiny insects to huge apes.

the emergent trees that are widely spaced, the trees of the canopy are close together. They are so close that, when viewed from above, their leaves appear to form a solid green ceiling.

The canopy is almost always warm because of the sunlight that strikes the leaves. With so much light and water absorbed through their roots, canopy trees carry out most of the photosynthesis that takes place in a tropical forest. As a result, canopy trees can grow to be huge. An example is a tree known as the great banyan that grows in the tropical forests of India. There, the canopy leaves of a great banyan spread out over more than 3 acres (1.2 ha).

Like all **organisms,** or living things, a banyan tree must have the **adaptations** to survive in its environment. An adaptation is any feature or behavior that increases an organism's chances of survival. In a tropical forest, the canopy prevents most sunlight from reaching the ground. As a result, canopy trees must have adaptations to survive with little or no sunlight until they are fully grown and tall enough to be part of the canopy.

The seed of a banyan tree does not sprout or start to grow on the ground. Instead, it begins its life high up in a tropical forest. The seed begins to germinate, or sprout, on one of the top branches of another tree on which it was most likely dropped by a bird. The seed gets the water it needs to sprout from raindrops. As the seed sprouts, roots start to grow toward the ground. These roots are thick enough to support

Seeking Shade

Alexander the Great reportedly had seven thousand of his soldiers rest under the shade of a single great banyan tree.

the tree until a trunk is formed. The banyan tree slowly strangles the tree on which it grows and eventually takes its place in the forest. With the full-grown tree standing almost 100 feet (30 m) tall, its leaves become part of the canopy and have no trouble getting enough sunlight and water.

A Dazzling Display

The sun-drenched canopy is rich in color. The leaves of canopy trees provide the green. But many canopy trees shed their leaves at certain times of the year and replace them with flowers. One of the most colorful displays is put on by silky oak trees, which are common in tropical forests. These trees, which can reach a height of more than 100 feet (30 m), produce red, gold, and orange flowers that grow in thick clusters. All of these colorful flowers attract insects seeking nectar.

A banyan tree can live for hundreds of years.

Orchids grow very slowly and cannot survive a dry spell.

Even more color is provided by a type of plant called an **epiphyte.** The word *epiphyte* comes from the Greek words *epi*, which means "upon," and *phyton*, which means "plant." Therefore, an epiphyte is a plant that grows upon another plant. Epiphytes depend on other plants, particularly trees, for support. Epiphytes use photosynthesis to make their own food. They obtain water from the moisture in the air and the raindrops that fall on the other plants.

Epiphytes that grow in a tropical forest include mosses, ferns, cacti, and orchids. One canopy tree may be home to more than two thousand epiphytes, including hundreds of cacti and orchids. A single cactus plant can produce a rainbow-colored flower as large as a person's head. A single orchid may produce eight colorful flowers, each as large as 6 inches (15 cm) in diameter.

Air Plants

Epiphytes are referred to as "air plants" because they grow high up in the tropical forest, far above the soil. In the canopy, epiphytes grow on the branches and trunks of trees and on vines. There are canopy plants that even grow on the leaves of other plants. These air plants are called epiphylls and flourish in high humidity.

More than twenty different kinds of epiphylls can grow on a single leaf. A leaf can become overburdened with epiphylls, which will use most of the available sunlight and water for photosynthesis. As a result, the leaf may die from its inability to manufacture enough food for itself. To prevent epiphylls from building up on them, leaves in a tropical forest usually have a waxy coating that causes water to run off them easily. The less water that accumulates on the leaves, the less likely it is that epiphylls will accumulate in large numbers.

The Understory

The layer beneath the canopy is known as the **understory.** Organisms in the understory are not exposed to the intense light, high winds, and heavy rains in the canopy. Rather, the canopy filters the light and rain. As a result, the understory is shady, warm, and moist.

The most common plants in the understory are palms. More than 2,500 different types of palms grow in tropical forests. The most common is the rattan palm. In fact, about two-thirds of the palms in some Asian tropical forests are rattans. These palms are common because of their highly successful adaptations. Rattans have spines and barbs on their

stems. Some even have long, whiplike structures. These spines, barbs, and whiplike structures help rattans climb trees. The higher they climb, the more sunlight they get.

Once at the top of the understory, a rattan palm may use its spines and barbs to spread to another tree. Rattans are such excellent climbers that they develop the longest stems of any plant in the world. The longest rattan stem on record measured more than 500 feet (152 m). Such long stems are prized because of their usefulness in making furniture.

These workers are making furniture using the stems of rattan plants. Between 80 and 85 percent of the rattan used to make furniture comes from Indonesian tropical forests.

A World Record

A palm produces a leaf that can reach a length of 65 feet (20 m), the longest of any plant in the world.

The Forest Floor

Very little sunlight reaches the forest floor, the lowest layer of a tropical forest. As a result, many plants that live in this layer have adaptations that allow them to survive without depending on photosynthesis to make their food. An example is the rafflesia plant that grows in Indonesia. The rafflesia produces the largest flower in the world, measuring about 3 feet (91 cm) across. The bud is about the size of a basketball and weighs about 35 pounds (16 kilograms). This plant has no leaves, stems, or roots.

Finding this plant is difficult because the flower remains open for only three days. It then dies and quickly decomposes. While the flower is open, it produces a terrible smell, like that of rotting meat. This smell attracts the flies that pollinate it so that new rafflesia plants can be produced.

The rafflesia plant survives at the expense of another plant. The entire rafflesia plant lives within the root or stem of a vine. Strands from the rafflesia penetrate the vine, from which it sucks out water and nutrients. The rafflesia is a **parasite,** an organism that benefits at the expense of another organism. As a parasite, rafflesia is one of the few flowering plants that are adapted to living on the tropical forest floor.

It takes about eighteen months for a rafflesia seed to produce a plant with a bud and another nine months for the bud to produce the flower you see in this photograph.

35

Gold prospectors, such as these men, have caused many animals to flee their tropical forest homes.

Chapter Four

Animals: From Bottom to Top

In addition to the crops they plant, the Yanomami also depend on the animals they hunt for food. They hunt with bows and arrows and with blowguns. With just these simple weapons, the Yanomami can kill large animals, such as wild pigs, monkeys, and wild turkeys. Their food source has dwindled, though, because of gold prospectors.

Until recently, between farming and hunting, the Yanomami had no trouble getting food. Today, gold prospectors have chased away most of the forest animals the Yanomami once hunted. Despite what has happened to the Amazon forest, a tropical forest is a place where a great diversity of animal life still exists.

The Forest Floor

With practically no sunlight and nutrient-poor soil, the forest floor is home to more animals than plants. Insects dominate the forest floor in terms of numbers. They include ants, termites, and beetles. One type of forest ant grows to be more than 1 inch (2.5 cm) long. These giant ants are aggressive. They paralyze their prey with a painful sting or bite. Although these ants mostly eat other insects, they have been

The Most Dangerous Insect

Malaria is a disease that one can easily get in a tropical forest. The World Health Organization estimates that between 300 and 500 million people develop malaria each year. More than one million of these people die. People get malaria from the bite of a mosquito that is infected with a parasite that causes the disease. Once in the blood, the parasite destroys red blood cells and causes fever, chills, headaches, and muscle aches. These symptoms usually appear from eight to twenty-five days after being bitten. An infected person can be treated with antimalarial drugs. Interestingly, one of the first drugs used to treat malaria was obtained from the bark of a tree that grows in a tropical forest.

known to attack much larger animals, including mice, frogs, lizards, and even humans. These ants travel in large numbers, often making enough noise to warn a possible target of the approaching danger.

With so many insects living on the tropical forest floor, it should be no surprise that **insectivores,** or insect eaters, are also common. One insectivore that lives in the African and Asian tropical forest is the pangolin. The pangolin is a **mammal,** which is an animal that has hair, can regulate its body temperature, and, in the case of females, produces milk. The pangolin is an unusual mammal because its body is not covered with hair but with scales, which are found on fish and reptiles.

The pangolin has short legs but huge claws. It uses its claws to dig into anthills and termite mounds. Once the insects are exposed, the pangolin projects its sticky tongue to pick up as many insects as possible. Insects must move quickly to avoid being eaten, as a pangolin's tongue can be as long as 16 inches (40 cm).

Large animals also inhabit the tropical forest floor, including jaguars, tigers, gorillas, and elephants. The jaguar is the largest member of the cat family in the tropical forests. With a body about 5 feet (1.5 m) long, it has a powerful build. A tail can add another 2 feet (0.6 m) to a jaguar's length. A

The pangolin is often mistaken for a reptile, as its scales look like those of a crocodile.

Jaguars once lived in the United States. One reason for their disappearance was overhunting for their fur.

Third-Largest

Jaguars are the third-largest cats in the world, following lions and tigers.

jaguar does not confine itself to the forest floor. When hunting for food, it may climb a tree to perch on a branch in the understory. It waits patiently until an animal passes by. The jaguar will suddenly drop to snare its victim, which may be an anteater, a monkey, an armadillo, or a porcupine. A jaguar will also stalk its victim and even swim in rivers to catch fish.

Tigers live in Asian tropical forests. A tiger can weigh as much as 550 pounds (250 kg) and usually feeds on animals that weigh more than 100 pounds (45 kg), including deer, wild pigs, and young elephants. When they are hungry, tigers will eat almost anything, including fish, birds, and occasionally humans who have accidentally wandered into their paths.

Tigers patiently stalk their victims on the forest floor. In a tropical forest, a tiger kills and consumes about one deer each week.

A gorilla rarely drinks because its gets all the water it needs from its food.

Gorillas, which inhabit African tropical forests, are shy, gentle, and peaceful creatures. A gorilla spends most of its day eating. Most gorillas are vegetarians, eating the leaves, stems, and fruits of plants. An adult male can weigh 600 pounds (272 kg) and may consume 65 pounds (29 kg) of vegetation every day. Most of their food comes from the forest floor, not from the trees.

Elephants are the largest tropical forest animal in Africa and Asia. An adult stands between 9 and 12 feet (2.7 and 3.7 m) at the shoulder and weighs between 8,000 and 12,000 pounds (3,629 and 5,443 kg). Elephants spend up to sixteen hours a day eating.

Like gorillas, elephants are vegetarians. Elephants use their large teeth to grind the tough plant matter they eat. When a tooth is worn down, a new one replaces it. An elephant will produce six sets of teeth during its lifetime. When the last set wears out, the elephant will no longer be able to eat and will die from starvation.

A female elephant has the longest pregnancy of any animal. It takes twenty-two months for a baby elephant to develop.

The Understory

Animals that live in the understory are very mobile. They can easily move from tree to tree in their search for food or shelter. Some animals, such as birds, bats, and bees, fly. Others, such as monkeys and frogs, jump. Still others, such as snakes and tarantulas, crawl through the understory.

One of the most unusual animals that fly through the understory is the vampire bat. These bats are found only in Central and South America. Vampire bats are about the size of an adult's thumb and have a wingspan of about 8 inches (20 cm). The vampire bat is the only mammal that feeds solely on blood.

A vampire bat uses special sensors in its nose to find a vein close to the skin of its victim.

On spotting a sleeping victim, a vampire bat flies in front of its face and then lands on the ground. The vampire bat then pounces on its victim and uses its sharp teeth to make a cut in its skin. The victim rarely wakes up.

Contrary to popular legend, a vampire bat does not suck blood from its victim. Rather, the bat's saliva contains a chemical that prevents the victim's blood from clotting. As the blood oozes from the cut, the vampire bat laps it up. Scientists have discovered that this chemical prevents blood clots better than any known medication. They are now investigating whether the saliva from the vampire bat can be used to prevent heart attacks and strokes.

Like vampire bats, snakes have also been the subject of myths and legends. But snakes are not that abundant in tropical forests. A person can walk for three or four days without ever spotting one. In addition, no snake attacks humans for food. Still, people must be careful should they come upon a poisonous snake, such as the blood python that lives in Asian tropical forests. Scientists who have worked in tropical forests say that a person has a greater chance of being harmed by a falling tree than of being bitten by a poisonous snake.

The Canopy

With all its leaves, the canopy offers a place for animals to hide themselves from their enemies. Until recently, scientists knew little about the animals that live in the canopy, simply because getting up there was almost impossible. Today, scientists

A Myth

Vampire bats usually feed on cows, pigs, and goats. Humans are not their favorite meal, although they do occasionally bite humans.

study animal life in the canopy by building towers and gently lowering bridges and rafts onto the treetops from the air.

Besides shelter, the canopy also offers its inhabitants a lot of food. Squirrel monkeys use their powerful legs to jump from tree to tree to feed on nuts, seeds, leaves, and insects. Flying squirrels search for fruits and nuts, while flying frogs consume insects. These squirrels and frogs do not actually fly. Instead, they have adaptations that allow them to glide through the air and control their fall.

Orangutans use twigs, vines, and leaves to build nests for sleeping in the canopy at night.

Perhaps the best-known of all the canopy animals are great apes: orangutans and chimpanzees. Orangutans are intelligent animals that live in the canopy, where they feed mainly on fruits. They depend on their intelligence to find ways of moving through the canopy, as they rarely descend to lower layers except in search of food. Their long arms, hands, and fingers help them climb. Orangutans were once found throughout Southeast Asia. But there are only between 15,000 and 25,000 orangutans living today on the islands of Borneo and Sumatra.

Chimpanzees are found only in African tropical forests, where they feed mainly on ripe fruits. Each morning they climb down from their nests in the canopy to search for food. Chim-

Chimpanzees live in groups called troops. Each troop consists of twenty-five to eighty chimpanzees.

panzees will sometimes hunt and kill small animals, such as young monkeys. Like orangutans, chimpanzees have become endangered. Fifty years ago, millions of chimpanzees lived in Africa. Today, scientists estimate that only about 150,000 chimpanzees remain.

The potential loss of the great apes is just one reason why so many people support efforts to save the world's remaining tropical forests. People realize that these forests are a valuable resource in many different ways. Unless the destruction of the world's remaining tropical forests stops, these resources may be lost forever.

So Much in Common

More than 98 percent of the genes in humans and chimpanzees are the same.

This rosy periwinkle plant grows only in the tropical forests of Madagascar. This plant is the only source of a drug used to treat leukemia and other types of cancer.

Chapter Five

A Valuable Resource

Perhaps as many as 100 million different kinds of organisms share Earth with us. Scientists estimate that between fifty and ninety million of them live in tropical forests. Many of these are found nowhere else on Earth. You have taken a look at just a few of these interesting plants and animals. As you have learned, the destruction of these forests has endangered the chances of survival of these and other organisms. Undoubtedly, many types of plants and animals have gone extinct even before they could be identified and studied.

A Most Productive Biome

You learned that plants carry out photosynthesis to produce food. Photosynthesis also produces oxygen and water. Because they have so many plants, tropical forests account for most of the water produced through photosynthesis worldwide. For example, a single emergent tree releases about 200 gallons (757 liters) of water into the atmosphere each day. One acre (0.405 ha) of tropical forest is estimated to release 20,000 gallons (75,708 l) of water every day. In comparison, only 1,000 gallons (3,785 l) of water evaporate each day from the same surface area of an ocean. Without tropical forests, far less water would be released into the atmosphere to form clouds. If fewer clouds are formed, areas throughout the world will receive less precipitation.

Scientists also estimate that 1 acre (0.405 ha) of tropical forest releases a little more than 11 tons of oxygen into the atmosphere each year. Tropical forest plants use much of the oxygen they produce to carry out **respiration,** just as animals do. But the plants produce more oxygen than they need, making the rest available for animals to use.

This tropical forest animal, known as a slow loris, depends on the oxygen produced by forest plants.

Just as important as the oxygen that tropical plants produce is the carbon dioxide they use to carry out photosynthesis. Tropical forest plants play a major role in removing carbon dioxide from the atmosphere before it can accumulate and contribute to global warming.

Foods and Medicines

Almost 80 percent of our food crops were domesticated from wild tropical forest plants. These include fruits such as bananas, tangerines, pineapples, apples, limes, lemons, grape-fruits, avocados, mangoes, plantains, papayas, coconuts, and oranges. Wild tropical forest plants were also the ancestors of domesticated vegetables such as yams, cabbage, brussels

Many of the fruits and vegetables sold in your supermarket were developed from tropical forest plants.

Chewing Gum

In 1869, an American inventor named Thomas Adams was experimenting with chicle, a saplike substance that comes from a tree in the Amazon. Adams was trying to make a substitute for rubber. He never succeeded. He did, however, find that his new product was fun to chew. This accidental discovery started a whole industry. Today, chewing gum is made from synthetic, rather than natural, ingredients. If you want to taste the original chewing gum, you may still find it in South America, where it is called chicle.

sprouts, barley, sugar beets, and broccoli. Spices such as cinnamon, nutmeg, paprika, vanilla, black pepper, and ginger also come from tropical forest plants. Other tropical forest foods include coffee, tapioca, chocolate, and peanuts.

Half the medicines we depend on come from plants, and half of these plants grow only in tropical forests. In other words, about 25 percent of the medicines used worldwide are based on chemical substances that were first found in tropical forest plants. These medicines are used as painkillers, muscle relaxants, and disease fighters.

To appreciate the value of just one plant, consider the cinchona tree, which is native to the Amazon. This tree grows to a height of 65 feet (20 m) and produces clusters of white, yellow, or pink fragrant flowers. In the 1640s, Spanish explorers noticed that natives of Peru used the bark of this tree to treat fevers. The bark was stripped from the tree, ground into a fine powder, mixed with water or wine, and then drunk.

The bark of the cinchona tree is still used to obtain quinine to treat the most dangerous form of malaria.

In 1820, two scientists isolated the active ingredient from the cinchona bark and called it quinine. Methods were soon developed to extract quinine from the bark. The extract was used to treat malaria. Today, doctors have a variety of drugs to treat malaria, a disease that affects as many as 500 million people worldwide. All these drugs have one thing in common: They were all made using quinine as a model. The cinchona tree has saved millions of lives. So have other plants that grow only in the tropical forest.

The Future

Since the 1990s, efforts have been made to increase public awareness about the threats to tropical forests. Some have

Other Uses

People in the Amazon also use quinine to treat indigestion and fatigue.

been quite successful. For example, the Rainforest Preservation Foundation was established in 1991. The goal of this organization is to buy and preserve forestland in the Amazon forest and to teach Brazilians to use better farming methods. To date, more than 8 million acres (3.24 million ha) have been protected.

Other efforts to increase public awareness include such events as races and concerts. In April 2004, the fourth annual Race for the Rainforest was held just outside a tropical forest in Costa Rica. That same year, the eleventh annual Rainforest Foundation benefit concert was held in New York City.

Even the Yanomami have tried to raise public awareness about the future of tropical forestlands. One of their leaders, Davi Kopenawa, has traveled around the world, speaking on behalf of his people and their land. In one speech, he said, "I want to speak giving the message from Omai. Omai is the creator of the Yanomami who also has created all the shaboris. The shaboris are the ones that have the knowledge, and they sent two of us to deliver their message. The message is to stop destruction, to stop taking out minerals from under the ground, to stop taking out the steel with which all the metal utensils are made, and to stop building roads through the forest. We feel that a lot of riches have already been taken out of the lands, and a lot of these riches are getting old and useless. Our work is to protect nature, the wind, the mountains, the forest, the animals, and this is what we want to teach you people."

Glossary

adaptation—a feature or behavior that increases an organism's chances of survival

atmosphere—the gases that surround a planet

biome—a geographic area in which environmental conditions determine the types of plants and animals that live there

canopy—the top layer of a tropical forest

epiphyte—a plant that grows on another plant

global warming—the gradual warming of Earth caused by gases in the atmosphere that trap heat energy from the Sun

insectivore—an organism that feeds on insects

mammal—an animal that has hair, regulates its body temperature, and, in the case of females, produces milk

nutrient—a substance a living thing needs to survive and grow

organism—a living thing

parasite—an organism that benefits at another organism's expense

photosynthesis—the process by which plants use light energy to make food

respiration—the process in which organisms use oxygen to obtain the energy stored in nutrients

tropical forest—a biome in which the climate includes high annual rainfall and warm temperatures all year

understory—the middle layer in a tropical forest

To Find Out More

Books

Ganeri, Anita. *Tropical Rainforests.* Columbus, Ohio: Peter Bedrick, 2001.

George, Michael. *Rainforests: Endangered Jewels.* Mankato, Minn.: Creative Education, 2003.

Johansson, Philip. *The Tropical Rain Forest: A Web of Life.* Berkeley Heights, N.J.: Enslow Publishers, 2004.

Oldfield, Sara. *Rainforest.* Cambridge, Mass.: MIT Press, 2003.

Ring, Susan. *Rain Forest Adventure.* Norwalk, Conn.: Innovative Kids, 2003.

Organizations and Online Sites

Journey into Amazonia

http://www.pbs.org/journeyintoamazonia/

Click on "Powerful Plants" to learn more about how tropical forest plants have been used. For example, in the days when ships depended on sails to cross oceans, these voyages were made possible by lashing the sails to the masts with a rope made from a fiber resistant to rot caused by saltwater. This fiber came from a tropical forest plant. Click on "Waterworlds" to explore the fascinating creatures that live in the Amazon rivers. One such animal is the red-bellied piranha, whose teeth can shred flesh from a bone in seconds. You can also play an interactive game called "Amazon Explorer."

Rainforest Alliance

665 Broadway, Suite 500

New York, NY 10012

http://www.rainforest-alliance.org

Learn how you can adopt a rain forest. This site also has numerous activities for students. Click on "Resources/Facts" to read some amazing but depressing facts about tropical forests.

Tropical Rainforest Animals

http://www.enchantedlearning.com/subjects/rainforest/animals/
Rfbiomeanimals.shtml

This book could only discuss a tiny number of animals that live in the tropical forest. Check out this site to learn about many more of these interesting creatures, such as the bongo, bonobo, and binturong.

Tropical Rainforest Foundation

http://www.ergocom-net.com/trf/intro.html

This foundation focuses on preserving the major tropical forest in North America—the Mayan Biosphere Reserve in Guatemala. You can read articles about what has been happening to this forest and check out the photo gallery. Based on current rates of deforestation, only 2 percent of the land will be covered with trees in 2010.

Yanomami: A Disappearing People

http://depts.clackamas.cc.or.us/banyan/3.1/yanomami.asp

Learn more about how the Yanomami lived in harmony with the tropical forest until others descended on their land. Read how theYanomami first felt the impact of foreigners in the middle of the 1800s.

A Note on Sources

My first introduction to tropical forests was Charles Darwin's *The Voyage of the Beagle.* On February 29, 1832, he recorded his first impression of the Brazilian forest: "The day has passed delightfully. Delight itself, however, is a weak term to express the feelings of a naturalist, who, for the first time, has wandered by himself in a Brazilian forest."

My first and main source in writing this book was Arnold Newman's *Tropical Rainforest.* Not surprisingly, Newman begins his book by quoting from Darwin's book: "The [Brazilian forest] is one great, wild, untidy, luxuriant hothouse, made by Nature for herself." In his book, Newman, like Darwin, gives the reader an appreciation of the beauty and value of the tropical forest. The Internet, as usual, provided additional information. But the first-hand knowledge gained while visiting the tropical forests in Central America was the most rewarding.

—*Salvatore Tocci*

Index

Numbers in *italics* indicate illustrations.

About the Author

Salvatore Tocci taught high school and college science for almost thirty years. He has a bachelor's degree from Cornell University and a master's degree from The City University of New York.

He has written books that deal with a range of science topics, from biographies of famous scientists to a high school chemistry textbook. He has also traveled throughout the United States to present workshops at national science conventions to show teachers how to emphasize the applications of scientific knowledge to students' everyday lives.

Tocci lives in East Hampton, New York, with his wife, Patti. One of their recent trips took them to tropical forests in Costa Rica, Guatemala, and Panama.